Wit & Humour

CATS

FELIX MOGG

To Mel,
Merry
Christmas
2015
love
Ardella x
A.K.A.
Felix
Mogg

BRADWELL
BOOKS

Published by Bradwell Books

9 Orgreave Close Sheffield S13 9NP

Email: books@bradwellbooks.co.uk

Compiled by Felix Mogg

All rights reserved. No part of this publication may be reproduced, stored in a retrieval
system or transmitted in any form or by any means, electronic, mechanical,
photocopying, recording or otherwise without the prior
permission of Bradwell Books.

British Library Cataloguing in Publication Data: a catalogue record
for this book is available
from the British Library.

1st Edition

ISBN: 9781910551264

Design by: Jenks Design

Illustrations: Tim O'Brien 2015

Print: Gomer Press, Llandysul, Ceredigion SA44 4JL

Owners of dogs will have noticed that, if you provide them with food and water and shelter and affection, they will think you are God. Whereas owners of cats are compelled to realise that, if you provide them with food and water and affection, they are God.

Two female cats are sitting on the front porch passing the time of day when a really handsome tom cat walks by and winks at them.

"Oh darling, did you see that one?" says one of the felines breathlessly.

"I wouldn't mind sharing a can of Cat-o-meat with him."
"Oh, forget about him, sweetie," says her friend. "I went out with him once, and all he did was talk about his operation."

Mrs. Brown was walking down the street one day carrying a small box with holes punched in the top.

"What's in that box?" Mrs. Green asked.
"A cat," Mrs. Brown answered.

"What for?" "I've been dreaming about mice at night, and I'm scared of them. The cat is to catch them."

"But the mice you dream about are imaginary," said Mrs. Green.
Mrs. Brown turned to her friend and whispered, "So is the cat."

A man absolutely hated his wife's cat and decided to get rid of him one day by driving him 5 miles from home and leaving him in the park. As he arrived home, the cat was walking up the driveway.

The next day he decided to drive the cat 10 miles away to the common. He put the beast out and headed home. Driving back up his driveway, there was the cat!

He kept taking the cat further and further, but the cat would always beat him home.

At last he decided to drive a few miles away, but try to confuse the cat. He drove off, then turned right, then left, round the roundabout, past the bridge, then right again and another right until he thought the cat would be totally bewildered. He opened the door and shoved the cat out onto the grass verge.

Hours later the man phoned home to his wife.

"Darling," he said, "is the cat there?"

"Yes," the wife answered, "why do you ask?"

"I need him to give me directions home," said the man, "I'm lost."

Little Tim was in the garden filling in a hole when his neighbour peered over the fence. Interested in what the child was up to, he asked, "Whatcha doing, Timmy?"

"My goldfish died," replied the boy tearfully, without looking up. "And I've just buried him."

The neighbor was concerned. "That's an awfully big hole for a goldfish, isn't it?" Tim patted down the last heap of earth then replied, "That's because he's inside your cat."

Q: What was the name of the actress cat's unauthorized biography?
A: Hiss and Tell.

John goes away for two months on a business trip to America and leaves his cat in his brother Jim's care. Three days before his return, he phones Jim.

"How's my cat doing?" he asks.

"He's dead", says Jim.

"He's dead!" says John, upset. "What do you mean 'He's Dead'! I loved that cat couldn't you think of a nicer way to tell me? You could have broken the news to me gently, in stages. I mean you could have started with, 'He's on the roof; we're having trouble getting him down. When I phoned you from the airport, you could have told me the Fire Brigade was there and they scared the cat off the roof. Then when I got home you could've said that he died when he hit the ground."

"I'm sorry," said Jim, "You're right...that was insensitive of me." "Alright, alright, forget about it," says John. "Anyway, how's Mum?"

"Well," said Jim, "She's on the roof; we're having trouble getting her down…"

Martha is walking in St. James' Park when she sees her friend Roger playing chess with his cat.

Martha says to Roger, "I can't believe what I'm seeing – a cat that plays chess. What a clever animal."

"Not that clever," says Roger, taking the cat's bishop, "I'm beating him six games to two."

"Some people say that cats are sneaky, evil, and cruel. True, and they have many other fine qualities as well." Anon.

Q: What do you call a cat with eight legs that likes to swim?
A: An octopuss.

Q: What do cat actors say on stage?
A: Tabby or not tabby

Q: What do you get if you cross a cat with a bottle of vinegar?

A: A sourpuss!

Q: Why did the judge dismiss the entire jury made up of cats?

A: Because each of them was guilty of purrjury.

Eight year-old Ben was at the corner shop picking out a large size box of laundry powder. The shopkeeper walked over, and, trying to be friendly, he asked the boy if he had a lot of laundry to do.

"Oh, not laundry," the boy said, "I'm going to wash my cat."

"But you shouldn't use this to wash your cat. It's very powerful and if you wash your cat in this, he'll get sick. In fact, it might even kill him."

Ben, however, was not to be persuaded and he carried the detergent to the counter and paid for it.

About a week later Ben was back in the shop to buy some sweets. The shopkeeper asked the boy how his cat was doing.

"Oh, he died," Ben said.

Trying to be kind, the shopkeeper said, "I am sorry your cat died but I did try to tell you not to use that detergent on him."

"Well," Ben replied, "I don't think it was the detergent that killed him."

"Oh? What was it then?" asked the man.

"I think it was the spin cycle," Ben replied.

The milkman was just about to leave two pints of semi-skimmed milk and some raspberry yoghurts on a doorstep when a cat popped its head out from under a rose bush. "My owner Mrs. Smith has gold-top," said the cat, "not semi-skimmed."

The milkman's mouth dropped open, the he muttered, "Thanks" and picked up the bottles of milk to change them.

"What are you doing?" came a woman's voice. It was Mrs. Smith returning from the shops. "Ignore that stupid cat. He knows perfectly well I'm on a diet."

Q: What does a cat do when it gets mad?

A: It has a hissy fit.

"To a cat, 'No' means 'Not while I'm looking.'" Anon.

Q: What do you get when you cross an elephant with a cat?

A: I don't know but watch out when it jumps up on your lap.

Q: Why was the cat so small?

A: Because it only drank condensed milk.

In front of the local pet shop, an antique collector noticed a mangy little kitten eating from a saucer. The saucer, he realised

with a start, was a rare and precious piece of Meissen porcelain – a valuable collector's item.

The man strolled into the shop and offered two pounds for the kitten.

"He's not for sale", said the shopkeeper.

"Look", said the collector, "that kitten is dirty and scabby, but I feel sorry for him.

I'll raise my offer to ten pounds."

"It's a deal", said the proprietor, and pocketed the tenner immediately.

"For that amount of money I'm sure you won't mind throwing in the saucer," said the connoisseur, "The kitten seems so happy drinking from it.'

"I can't do that," said the shopkeeper firmly, "That's my lucky saucer.
From that saucer, I've sold 18 cats already this week."

Q: What is a cat's favorite colour?

A: Purrr-ple

Q: Why did the cat put oil on the mouse?

A: Because it squeaked.

Q: Have you ever seen a catfish?

A: No. How did he hold the rod and reel?

A cat turns up for a job interview and is asked, "Can you speak any foreign languages?"

"Woof," she replied

A performing cat has been signed up to star in a Hollywood kids' movie.

"Anything you need?" says the producer, "We'll do anything to make you comfy."

"Well," says the cat, "I would like some satin cushions in my trailer."

"You got them!" says the producer.

Also working in the film are a troupe of mice dancing on roller-skates and a rat on a skateboard.

A few days pass and the producer checks that his leading cat is OK.

"Did you like the satin cushions?" he asks.

"Yes, thanks," says the cat. "Very comfy and the meals on wheels thing is a really nice touch."

A lady had a beautiful black cat called Midnight who spent his days outside and his nights indoors. One crisp autumn evening he disappeared and the lady searched for him in vain.

The following spring, Midnight reappeared, looking plump, his coat glossy and sleek.

The lady decided he must have been sowing his wild oats. Everything went back to normal until next autumn when he disappeared again. The lady was very worried but that spring he turned up again looking happy and well.

The lady was perplexed and went round to all the neighbours asking if they'd been feeding Midnight during the winter. Eventually she rang the doorbell of the biggest house in the village and an imperious old woman answered. "Have you by any chance been feeding a black cat during the winter?" asked Midnight's owner.

"Feeding him?" exclaimed the lady of the house, "I put him in a cat box every October and take him on holiday to the Caribbean!"

"Dogs come when they're called. Cats take a message and get back to you later." – Mary Bly

Q: Why did the cat cross the road?
A: It was the chicken's day off.

Q: What kind of kitten works for the Red Cross?

A: A first-aid Kit.

Q: What do you get if you cross a cat and a gorilla?

A: An animal that puts you out a night.

A salesman dropped in to see a business customer. Not a soul was in the office except a cat emptying wastepaper baskets. The salesman stared at the animal, wondering if his imagination could be playing tricks on him. The cat looked up and said, "Don't be surprised. This is just part of my job."

"Incredible!" exclaimed the man. "I can't believe it! Does your boss know what a prize he has in you? A cat that can talk! I must tell him!"

"No, no," pleaded the cat. "Please don't! If he finds out I can talk, he'll make me answer the phones as well!"

Q: What works in a circus, walks a tightrope and has claws?
A: An acrocat.

Q: What is the difference between a cat and a comma?
A: One has the paws before the claws and the other has the clause before the pause.

A man in the cinema notices what looks like a Siamese cat sitting next to him.

"Are you a cat?" asks the man, surprised.

"Yes," says the Siamese.

"What are you doing watching a movie?" asks the man.

"Well, I liked the book," the Siamese replies.

Q: What is a cat's way of keeping law & order?

A: Claw Enforcement.

Lady at lunch: "My husband said it was him or the cat... I miss him sometimes."

Q: Who helped Cinderella's cat go to the ball?

A: Her furry godmother.

"Cat's motto: No matter what you've done wrong, always try to make it look like the dog did it."

Q: What's a cat's favorite dessert?

A: Chocolate mouse!

Q: What do you call a cat that has just eaten a whole duck?

A: A duck-filled fatty puss.

Q: What is white, sugary, has whiskers and floats on the sea?

A: A catameringue.

"Dogs have owners; cats have staff." Anon.

Q: Did you hear about the cat who swallowed a ball of wool?
A: She had mittens.

Q: Did you hear about the cat that climbed the Himalayas?
A: She was a sher-paw.

Q: What do you get if you cross a cat with a tree?

A: A cat-a-logue!

Q: If there are ten cats on a boat and one jumps off, how many cats are left on the boat?

A: None – they were copycats.

A lady had a pet parrot called Mimi, that she loved very much, who talked and sat on her shoulder. One morning she woke up, went to the bathroom, came out, and realised that Mimi wasn't on her shoulder. She found her lying on her back under her perch. She called her name, but she didn't get up or speak. So the lady took her to the vet.

The vet looked at her parrot and said, "I'm afraid, your parrot is dead."

"Are you sure?" she cried. "I want you to double-check."

The vet went into the next room, and came back with a cage with a cat in it. He let a cat out, and she walked around the parrot, sniffed, looked at the vet and said, "Miaow!" Then she went back in her cage. The doctor put the cage back in the other room, came back and repeated, "Your parrot is dead."

"I can't believe it!" cried the lady, "Please, do another test."

So the vet went into the next room and came back with a Labrador on a lead. The Labrador walked around poor Mimi, sniffing, then looked at the vet and shook its head.

"I'm afraid," said the vet to the lady, "Your parrot is definitely dead."

"Poor Mimi!" cried the lady, stifling a sob, "OK, how much do I owe you?"

The vet said, "£500."

"What!?!?" exclaimed the lady, "How could it cost that much to tell me my parrot is dead?"

"Well," said the doctor, "It's only £15.00 for me to pronounce it dead but you insisted on the CAT scan and the Lab test."

Q: What do cats use to make coffee?

A: A purrcolator.

"The cat could very well be man's best friend but would never stoop to admitting it." Doug Larson

The Guide Dog charity ran out of dogs so they had to give the blind man a guide cat.

"Are you sure a cat can do the job?" asked the blind man.

"Of course," said the lady from the charity, "She's an exceptionally clever cat."

Two days later the lady got a call from the Fire Brigade who had had to rescue the blind man from the top of a tree. "Where was his guide cat?" she asked.

"In the park wearing the poor guy's dark glasses and throwing his white stick for a dog," said the Fire Chief.

Q: How does the cat get its own way?

A: With friendly purrsuasion.

Q: How many cats can you put into an empty box?

A: Only one – after that, the box isn't empty.

Q: Did you hear about the cat who drank 5 bowls of milk?

A: He set a new lap record.

Q: What is a cat's favourite movie?

A: The Sound of Mewsic.

Q: What do cats read in the morning?

A: Mewspapers.

"Cats took many thousands of years to domesticate humans." Anon.

A couple were getting ready to go out for the evening. They turned on a night light, switched the answering machine on, covered up the budgie's cage and put the cat out in the backyard. They phoned for a taxi. When it arrived, the couple opened the front door to leave but the cat scooted back into the house.

"That cat's after the budgie," said the husband, running after it in hot pursuit.

The wife didn't want the taxi-driver to know the house would be empty so she went over to the cab and said, "My husband will be out soon. He's just going upstairs to say goodbye to my mother."

A few minutes later, the husband gets into the Taxi. "Sorry I took so long," he said, as they drove away. "The stupid bitch was hiding under the bed. I had to poke her with a coat hanger to get her to come out. Then I had to wrap her in a blanket to keep her from scratching me and throw her out into the back yard!"

Q: What is a cat's favourite car?

A: The Catillac.

Q: What do cat's drink when they feel run down?

A: Catatonic.

A woman brought her two cats in to the veterinary clinic for their annual checkup. One was a small- framed, round tiger-striped tabby, while the other was a long, sleek black cat. She watched closely as the vet put each on the scale. "They weigh about the same," he told her.

"That proves it!" she exclaimed. "Black does make you look slimmer. And stripes make you look fat."

Q: How do you know when your cat has been using your computer?
A: When your mouse has teeth marks on it!

Q: What do cats like to eat for breakfast?
A: Mice Krispies.

Q: What's happening when you hear "Woof... splat... meow... splat?"
A: It's raining cats and dogs.

My kitten was having trouble watching a DVD, turns out she just had the movie on paws.

A rich woman died and left most of her fortune to her cat.

"I don't understand it," said her husband to the lawyer, "Why did she love that cat more than me? I know I wasn't the perfect husband but the cat never listened to her either; it didn't come home when she called; it often stayed out all night, and when it was home it just ate and slept. I don't see how the cat was any different to me." He sighed and asked sadly. "And who got the rest of her money?"

"The vet," said the lawyer.

Q: What's worse than raining cats and dogs?

A: Hailing taxi cabs.

Q: How do cats end a fight?

A: They hiss and make up.

Q: Why did the cat run from the tree?

A: Because it was afraid of the bark!

Q: What happened when the cat went to the flea circus?

A: She stole the show!

Q: Where did the hippycat go to find himself?

A: Catmando.

Q: Why was the cat so grumpy?

A: He was in a bad mewed.

Q: What do you call it when you keep thinking that your cat is up to no good?

A: Purranoia.

Q: What is the cat's favorite magazine?

A: Good Mousekeeping.

Q: What is the cat's favorite TV show?

A: The evening mews.

Q: What kind of cats purr the best?

A: Purrrrr-sians!

Q: What is the best award a cat can earn?

A: The Purr-litzer prize

"Cats are rather delicate creatures and they are subject to a good many ailments, but I never heard of one who suffered from insomnia." Joseph Wood Krutch

Q: What did the cat do when he swallowed some cheese?

A: He waited by the mouse hole with baited breath.

Q: What does a cat like to rest its head on?

A: A caterpillar.

Q: What do you call a cat that lives in an igloo?

A: An eskimew!

Q: Where is one place that your cat can sit, but you can't?

A: Your lap.

Q: What's furry, has whiskers and chases outlaws?

A: A posse cat

Q: Why happened when the cat swallowed a coin?

A: There was some money in the kitty.

Q: Why do cats chase birds?

A: For a lark

Q: What do you use to comb a cat?

A: A catacomb.